HumaniTrees

Exploring Human Nature through the Spirit of Trees

HumaniTrees

Exploring Human Nature through the Spirit of Trees

Joan Klostermann-Ketels

FINDHORN PRESS

The right of Joan Klostermann-Ketels to be identified as the author
of this work has been asserted by her in accordance with the
Copyright, Designs and Patents Act 1998.

Published in 2011 by Findhorn Press, Scotland

ISBN 978-1-84409-544-5

A CIP record for this title is available from the British Library.

Cover & interior design by Damian Keenan
Photography by Joan Klostermann-Ketels

The quote by Nalini Nadkarni on page 7
is reprinted with permission of the author.

Printed and bound in the European Union

1 2 3 4 5 6 7 8 9 17 16 15 14 13 12 11

Published by
Findhorn Press
117-121 High Street,
Forres IV36 1AB,
Scotland, UK

t +44 (0)1309 690582
f +44 (0)131 777 2711
e info@findhornpress.com

www.findhornpress.com

DEDICATION

TO MY HUSBAND, *Denton*, whose talents, gifts, vision, heart and soul are beyond measure. I treasure every single moment and breath we get to share together in this life. I love you, boss.

And to my parents—*Art Klostermann*, whose spirit, respect for the land, and incredible love of trees live on in all of his children and grand-children; and *Verna Klostermann*, whose actions, steadiness and unshakeable faith leave me in complete and utter awe of this woman, my mother. Her strength can only be matched by the size of her heart.

NOTE FROM THE AUTHOR

WE LIVED ON A FARM ten miles from the nearest town. Our lane was nearly a mile long. I was nine or ten years old at the time, the middle child in a family of twelve. It wasn't that we were completely isolated but we certainly weren't surrounded by people either.

The attack came suddenly and without warning. I can't remember who was attacking us or why. I only knew that they were hunting my family and me like dogs. My first instinct was to climb the large oak tree that stood guard beside our house. The leaves had fallen and the branches were bare, but hiding in this massive tree seemed like the most obvious option. As I snuggled in behind one of the enormous branches something surreal seemed to happen. I remember feeling as though I had become part of the tree.

I looked down and watched as my parents and siblings ran for cover. One by one as they came close to the tree, they were somehow safely transported to a branch of their own. I was most concerned about my brother, Ricky, who has Down syndrome. I tried to get his attention as he stood by the tree wondering what was happening. Suddenly he was there beside me and I hung onto him with all my might. I looked around the tree and somehow my entire family had all found a place in the various branches of this glorious oak tree—this sentry, this protector of our family. The relief I felt was beyond words. But the attackers still were below us, looking baffled and confused. At one point one of them looked up into the tree. I thought for sure he had seen us. He looked up briefly and then walked away.

It was at this point—every night for nearly a year—that I woke up. I woke up frightened yet feeling overwhelmingly grateful. Of course, I had to make my nightly trek through the house to make sure that everyone survived the ordeal. And before heading back to bed, I'd walk to the window and look outside where that big oak tree stood to say thank you.

The lifelong connection I have felt with trees must have begun with this recurring dream. I guess I never really thought much about it. This much I do know, I have felt the healing energy and protective power of trees ever since I was a young child. That I have over the years taken photographs of trees showing human emotions and conditions just seems right somehow. It's my way of honoring these magnificent spirits and their place on our planet.

I know there are thousands of people around the world who feel this connection to trees. Nalini Nadkarni, National Geographic Speaker and President of the International Canopy Network, describes our connection to trees this way:

> *"No matter the species, trees are a universal connector to the human condition. Trees breathe life, they give life, they support other growing and living organisms — much like humans. Trees have trunks. Humans have trunks. Trees have limbs. Humans have limbs… It wasn't a coincidence that the Old Testament had 328 references to trees and forests, explaining they are the very root of life."*

Walk with me…

ENLIGHTENED

"I don't pretend to understand the Universe –
it's a great deal bigger than I am."

— THOMAS CARLYLE —

INTREPID

"Valor is stability, not of legs and arms,
but of courage and the soul."

— MICHEL DE MONTAIGNE —

PROUD

"Dignity does not consist in possessing honors,
but in deserving them."

— ARISTOTLE —

DISCREET

"He that would live in peace and at ease must not
speak all he knows or all he sees."

— BENJAMIN FRANKLIN —

SHY

———

"The awareness of our own strength
makes us modest."

— PAUL CEZANNE —

PRIMAL

"Instinct is untaught ability."

— ALEXANDER BAIN —

POISED

"…waiting for the spark from heaven to fall."

— MATTHEW ARNOLD —

OTHERWORLDLY

"Every beauty which is seen here by persons of perception
resembles more than anything else that celestial source
from which we all are come."

— MICHELANGELO —

BOISTEROUS

"There is nothing stable in the world;
uproar's your only music."

— JOHN KEATS —

HAPPY-GO-LUCKY

"Fan the sinking flame of hilarity with the wing
of friendship; and pass the rosy wine."

— CHARLES DICKENS —

CAPTIVATED

"The price of anything
is the amount of life
you exchange for it."

— HENRY DAVID THOREAU —

GRATEFUL

———————

"Keep your eyes open to your mercies.
The man who forgets to be thankful
has fallen asleep in life."

— ROBERT LOUIS STEVENSON —

CAREFREE

———

"He does not seem to me to be a free man who
does not sometimes do nothing."

— MARCUS TULIUS CICERO —

ENIGMATIC

"The charm of history and its enigmatic lesson
consist in the fact that, from age to age,
nothing changes and yet everything
is completely different."

— ALDOUS HUXLEY —

SLEEPY

"A life of leisure and a life of laziness are two things.
There will be sleeping enough in the grave."

— BENJAMIN FRANKLIN —

Photo by
Bob Long

DEVOTED

———◈◆◈———

"Love is composed of a single soul
inhabiting two bodies."

— ARISTOTLE —

PEOPLE YOUNG AND OLD are drawn to trees. Throughout our lives we remain fascinated by the aesthetic beauty of these dynamic sculptures of nature. We feel their spiritual energy. We sense their wisdom.

Who among us has not found calmness in the way their delicate branches respond to a summer breeze, or been thrilled at the fiery show of color in autumn? What child does not find comfort beneath a huge oak tree—or rush to climb limbs their mothers would think too high? Never mind that their mothers climbed the same tree when they were young.

Trees seem to make their strongest appeals to the human spirit when the leaves have fallen away from their bones. Faces of bark and fiber that have been hidden all summer suddenly laugh out loud and bellow their lust for life. The spaces between the branches reveal the spirit beneath the camouflage, reminding us that without spaces in our own lives we may miss the most important and poignant moments.

When listening to beautiful music, it's not the running together of notes but the rests between them that make one gasp. In dance, it's the small, almost imperceptible pauses during the waltz that make one appreciate the beauty of the dancers' movement. The rhythm of our lives seems also to plead for these spaces, these moments of quiet reflection. And our bodies are designed to let us know what season we are in and when it is time for space in our lives.

Trees are great teachers of time, space and transition. When we quiet ourselves enough to see and feel the spaces, we might also notice that trees can show us how to live, how to celebrate, how to accept pain, and yes, even how to die—all with a sense of dignity, honor and place—if we let them.

HERE

All we have is this moment

That's

it

That's

all

— JOAN KLOSTERMANN KETELS —

POMPOUS

"None are so empty
as those who are full of themselves."

— BENJAMIN WHICHCOTE —

FATHERLY

———◆◆◆———

"There is frequently more to be learned
from the unexpected questions of a child
than the discourses of men."

— JOHN LOCKE —

COY

"How strange that Nature does not knock,
and yet does not intrude!"

— EMILY DICKINSON —

BOSSY

"Be the chief but never the lord."

— LAO TZU —

HUNGRY

"Nature has planted in our minds an
insatiable longing to see the truth."

— MARCUS TULLIUS CICERO —

VICTORIOUS

"A great pleasure in life is doing what
people say you cannot do."

— WALTER BAGEHOT —

PRESIDENTIAL

"Every individual has a place to fill in the world
and is important in some respect whether
he chooses to be so or not."

— NATHANIEL HAWTHORNE —

GRUMPY

———⋯———

"Some people are always grumbling because
roses have thorns; I am thankful that
thorns have roses."

— ALPHONSE KARR —

EFFUSIVE

"Exuberance is beauty."

—WILLIAM BLAKE —

ANGELIC

"To love for the sake of being loved is human,
but to love for the sake of loving
is angelic."

— ALPHONSE DE LAMARTINE —

FRAZZLED

"A well-adjusted person is one who makes the same
mistake twice without getting nervous."

— ALEXANDER HAMILTON —

SISTERLY

"We often have to put up with most from those
on whom we most depend."

— BALTASAR GRACIAN —

OBSERVANT

"The true spirit of conversation consists in
building on another man's observation,
not overturning it."

— ROBERT BULWER-LYTTON —

BLIND FAITH

Seems to me
I had a much better grasp of
life
when I was a kid

Everything just seemed to make sense –
I had a purpose for
being here

All of the big questions
I have now
made sense back then
somehow

I trusted the universe
to take care of me
because I didn't know
any better

And the God we humans
so desperately
want to know and love and trust was just
part of me

It was a feeling of complete
and utter safety and
unconditional love

And if I ever
for one second
questioned that

All I had to do was lay down in the grass
under my favorite tree and
look to the stars

And life was good

No questions
no doubts
just unadulterated trust and faith
in something

Way bigger than me…

— JOAN KLOSTERMANN KETELS —

CURIOUS

"You must not know too much, or be too precise
or scientific about birds and trees and flowers.
A certain free margin …
helps your enjoyment of these things"

— WALT WHITMAN —

DOUBTFUL

—◆◈◆—

"Doubt is not a pleasant condition,
but certainty is absurd."

— VOLTAIRE —

ENCHANTED

"Nature is the art of God."

— DANTE ALIGHIERI —

SERENE

"He who would be serene and pure
needs but one thing,
detachment."

— MEISTER ECKHART —

STUNNED

———

"You get tragedy where the tree,
instead of bending,
breaks."

— LUDWIG WITTGENSTEIN —

IMPISH

―――――――――

"You can discover more about a person
in an hour of play
than in a year of conversation."

— PLATO —

SHOW OFF

"There is an optical illusion
about every person we meet."

— RALPH WALDO EMERSON —

AGILE

"A man who as a physical being
is always turned toward the outside,
thinking that his happiness lies outside him,
finally turns inward and discovers that
the source is within him."

— SOREN KIERKEGAARD —

UNTAMED

"Nature is not human hearted."

— LAO TZU —

ASPIRING

"We live in an ascending scale when we live happily,
one thing leading to another in an endless series."

— ROBERT LOUIS STEVENSON —

DUTIFUL

———— ✦ ————

"I will act as if what I do makes a difference."

— WILLIAM JAMES —

DRAMATIC

"My advice to you concerning applause is this:
enjoy it but never quite believe it."

— SAMUEL LOVER —

WHIMSICAL

———◆◆◆———

"Life is like music;
it must be composed by ear, feeling, and instinct,
not by rule."

— SAMUEL BUTLER —

OBSESSED

"In order to properly understand the big
picture, everyone should fear becoming
mentally clouded and obsessed
with one small section of truth."

— XUN ZI —

HAND OF GOD

"Live your life, do your work,
then take your hat."

— HENRY DAVID THOREAU —

PASSIONATE

"You can't reason with your heart;
it has its own laws,
and thumps about things which
the intellect scorns."

— MARK TWAIN —

MISCHIEVOUS

"There are but very few men clever enough
to know all the mischief they do."

— FRANCOIS DE LA ROCHEFOUCAULD —

SPELLBOUND

"You have been trapped in the inescapable
net of ruin by your own want of sense."

— AESCHYLUS —

STUBBORN

———◆◆◆———

"Many are stubborn in pursuit of the path they have chosen,
few in pursuit of the goal."

— FRIEDRICH NIETZSCHE —

AGONIZED

"…I sensed an infinite scream passing
through nature."

— EDVARD MUNCH —

WILY

"Self-interest is but the survival of the animal in us.
Humanity only begins for man
with self-surrender."

— HENRI FREDERIC AMIEL —

CONNECTED

"In nature we never see anything isolated, but everything
in connection with something else which is before it,
beside it, under it and over it."

— JOHANN WOLFGANG VON GOETHE —

ORNERY

❦

"Make yourself an honest man, and then you may
be sure there is one less rascal in the world."

— THOMAS CARLYLE —

ATTENTIVE

"Genius is nothing but continued attention."

— CLAUDE ADRIEN HELVETIUS —

BRAVE

———◆◆◆———

"The whole secret of existence is to have no fear."

— BUDDHA —

CLUSMY

"I never saw an ugly thing in my life:
for let the form of an object be what it may,
– light, shade, and perspective
will always make it beautiful."

— JOHN CONSTABLE —

DANGEROUS

———◆———

"The serpent, the king, the tiger, the stinging wasp,
the small child, the dog owned by other people, and the fool:
these seven ought not to be awakened from sleep."

— CHANAKYA —

RADIANT

"Nature is an infinite sphere
of which the center is everywhere
and the circumference nowhere."

— BLAISE PASCAL —

NOCURNAL

"I often think that the night is more alive
and more richly colored than the day."

— VINCENT VAN GOGH —

RELAXED

───◆◆◆───

"It is a requisite for the relaxation of the mind
that we make use, from time to time,
of playful deeds and jokes."

— SAINT THOMAS AQUINAS —

RELENTLESS

"It's easier to resist at the beginning
than at the end."

— LEONARDO DA VINCI —

SURPRISED

———◆◆◆◆———

"Chance is always powerful.
Let your hook always be cast;
in the pool where you least expect it,
there will be a fish."

— OVID —

AWAKENED

"Compared to what we ought to be,
we are half awake."

— WILLIAM JAMES —

PURPOSEFUL

"And this, our life, exempt from public haunt,
finds tongues in trees, books in the running brooks,
sermons in stones, and good in everything."

— WILLIAM SHAKESPEARE —

WHOO-HOO!

"Great is the man who has not lost his childlike heart."

— MENCIUS —

SATISFIED

"Well done is better than well said."

— BENJAMIN FRANKLIN —

MIGHTY

"It is unwise to be too sure of one's own wisdom.
It is healthy to be reminded that the strongest
might weaken and the wisest might err."

— MOHANDAS GANDHI —

BEST FRIENDS

"I have learned that to be with those I like
is enough."

— WALT WHITMAN —

GENEROUS

———— ⋅◦✦◦⋅ ————

"That best portion of a man's life, his little, nameless,
unremembered acts of kindness and love."

— WILLIAM WORDSWORTH —

HOW WE NAMED OUR HUMANITREES
GALLERY OF TREE SPIRITS

*Everyone sees something different. What you see is the essence of the **Humani-Trees** exercise. What follows is the rationale we applied in naming these characters. They are but one way of interpreting these tree spirits. At the end of this list is a short guide to applying criteria for your own discussions of these images, or of the tree spirits you encounter in your own outdoor adventures. What you discover about nature, and your own perceptions of it, may surprise and amuse you.*

ENLIGHTENED P.8: Bending back, arms outstretched as if in celebration of a sudden and unexpected (aren't they all?) epiphany, this forest dweller accepts the full warmth and light of the winter sun. There is a feeling of gratitude, well-being and overwhelming happiness in its presence.

INTREPID P.10: It stands on the ridge in fearless anticipation of another great day on the frontier outpost. There is nothing this adaptable creature has not seen and nothing it cannot survive.

PROUD P.12: Stout, weathered and facing the light, this tree makes its stand with all the pride of an eagle and the alertness of a hawk. As with so many venerable characters, we feel a comfortable assurance that something great is here, a higher consciousness present on a different plane, to be sensed but not accessed, for we are not equipped to understand. Like so many peoples and cultures before us, we are free to ignore it, acknowledge it, respect it and worship it.

DISCREET P.14 : Two friends meet in the distance; an intimate conversation is taking place. Whatever the reason for having carefully chosen their surroundings for this meaningful and *discreet* encounter, their desire for privacy is acknowledged and respectfully granted by the other spiritual residents of this peaceful area.

SHY P.16 : "I'm cute! She said I'm cute!"

PRIMAL P.18 : One of the most incredible trees we've ever seen, and one that could only be viewed at this angle by boat. At first we perceived that this vain, nymph-like creature was enticing us to come closer. But why? Perhaps only to enjoy her ritualistic, ceremonial dance high above the marshy floor of the woods at the far end of the lake. She is celebrating her *primal* essence.

POISED P.20 : Strong trunk, strong arms, self-confident, athletic and capable. If you want something done in this particular area of nature, you could ask this individual tree and be confident that it will be accomplished most expeditiously…which is to say, in due time.

OTHERWORLDLY P.22 : An ethereal spirit materializes from the vapors of early morning, its branches nearly indistinguishable among the extravagant tangle on the opposite riverbank.

BOISTEROUS P.24 : Crazy hat, loud mouth, you gotta' love him. *Go Trees!* It's Homecoming at HumaniTrees U!

HAPPY-GO-LUCKY P.26 : A bit cockeyed and leaning to one side, this one goes through life in a state of constant amazement with its surroundings. There might be a little attention deficit at work here, but if it helps with acceptance who's to say it's a disorder?

CAPTIVATED P.28 : This character seems resigned to her shipwrecked state…out on a limb, tortured by her passions. Then again she may be perfectly fine with it. Either way, she is *captivated*.

GRATEFUL P.30: We find this spirit paying homage to the One Great Spirit who grants the gift of the elements and energy. We are humbled and reminded of our own gratitude, so frequently lost in the speed and superficiality of our days.

CAREFREE P.32: He doesn't even know we're there. Or rather, he doesn't care. He's just having fun, enjoying the beautiful day by making snow angels in the leaves. He is laughing out loud and utterly *carefree*.

ENIGMATIC P.34: Our friends have seen in this beautiful tree an embryo, the man in the moon, a figure in a monastic robe, two high-spirited individuals having an intense discussion and countless other characters and events. It is, perhaps more than any other image captured in this collection, *enigmatic*.

SLEEPY P.36: It might have been a rough night in the woods, or maybe this tree is not an early riser. Either way, our friend Bob Long caught this fellow working on a major league yawn and shared the picture with us.

DEVOTED P.38: This sweet old couple has but a short time left in their present form, and they are spending it in celebration of their life and time here together. It is the ultimate Anniversary Waltz, perhaps their 50th, 75th or maybe 100th. It will endure forever in spirit, in the eternal now.

POMPOUS P.42: The forest's politician has a lot of ideas and he's not afraid to beller on about them. Now, this could also be a baritone letting loose his woodsian opera titled, "This Beautiful Autumn Day Will Never Be Repeated." Again, you see what you see when you see it.

FATHERLY P.44: Pointing to a hill afar, the *fatherly* tree shares historical knowledge, legend and the philosophy behind it all to his son, who is reaching out enthusiastically below. This is a touching and intimate moment indeed.

COY P.46: He knows he's adorable, and plays peek-a-boo with every trail walker that comes along. He'd be disappointed if we didn't notice.

BOSSY P.48: Popping up like a mysterious apparition, this caped stranger authoritatively points the way through a section of the woods with which we are largely unfamiliar. He knows all, sees everything and is obviously in charge around these parts. On the other hand, he might just be umpiring a friendly game of spring softball... "You're out!"

HUNGRY P.50: Any time is lunchtime for this big guy, and he has an appetite that befits his thick frame. Today's fare is pasta, and he's really enjoying that noodle he's slurping up over his thick lower lip. Hey, everybody's gotta' eat. Mmmm...spaghetti.

VICTORIOUS P.52: Hands raised in victory as if signaling a touchdown, this staunch and dependable being has done far more than simply survive. It has prevailed over the elements and spends every moment enjoying the spoils. Like a trusted leader, coach or spiritual advisor, this being enthusiastically encourages us to settle for nothing less than to enjoy life right now. We are happy in its presence.

PRESIDENTIAL P.54: The salute, the resolute demeanor and, of course, the hair—there is no mistaking the resemblance to the 40th President of the United States of America, Ronaldus Magnus. It's morning in the forest.

GRUMPY P.56: Hey. So I'm not the best looking guy in the world. What do you want from me?

EFFUSIVE P.58: Emoting in all directions, carrying on simultaneous conversations, this character leaves nothing on the table. An enthusiastic multi-tasker.

ANGELIC P.60: Snow on the wings accentuates the heavenly pose of this gentle creature who seems ready to take flight at any moment. Then again, she may just fall backward to make a playful impression of herself in the wintry cover.

FRAZZLED P.62: Circumstances of life, nearly all of which is out of her control, give an outer appearance of a being who is rather *frazzled*. Nevertheless, she is growing straight and tall irrespective of the relentless distractions. The longer we contemplate this condition, it may well be more the perfect picture of one who is, above all, *accepting* of everything and everyone making demands of—or relying on—her. We would have renamed it but for nature's lesson that one's true spiritual condition is not always what it outwardly seems.

SISTERLY P.64: Inseparable, strong and completely committed to each other's well being, we could not shake the feeling that big sister on the right sometimes grows weary of little sister's incessant curiosity and her need to tag along.

OBSERVANT P.66: Eyes always open, the friendly observer sees all. What it doesn't see, it gets from the woodpeckers who reside in its head.

CURIOUS P.70: Childlike in appearance, with bright eyes and a little pointed Pinocchio-like nose (no lies for this tree), it is the picture of innocence and a willingness to learn all about what's going on in the woods around it. Can the two states coexist for long?

DOUBTFUL P.72: Inquisitive and a bit on the skeptical side, this thoughtful being is constantly considering all the possibilities. He never really arrives at an answer—he doesn't accept and doesn't reject a position—he just continuously ponders. It's his spiritual lot in life, and he rather enjoys the constant re-evaluation of things. He wears out most of the other woodland conversationalists. He is thinking about running for Mayor of the woods, but hasn't positively arrived at a decision. It may not be such a good idea.

ENCHANTED P.74: Peeling off his cartoonish outer costume, this spirit's real persona is visible beneath. Perhaps he's just going home after another long day in the *enchanted* forest, this particular one of which is in Colorado.

SERENE P.76: Standing proudly, driven to survive through its natural ability and optimism, this lovely tree occupies a place frequented by human grief, sorrow, joy and celebration, and says in its *serene* way, "All is fundamentally well."

STUNNED P.78: "*Ouch*! Holy…! What?! I finally get it! Hey you guys, come here! I've got something to tell you!"

IMPISH P.80: We saw her from the boat, peeking out at us with her tiny face. Hard telling what she's up to, but we haven't had a decent bite all day. Could she be in league with the bass and wily catfish?

SHOW OFF P.82: There's one in every crowd.

AGILE P.84: We were struck with how much this tree—or piece of a tree—resembled a Star Wars or Avatar character. With its small head and athletic long legs, it appears to be 'on guard' and protective of something, perhaps aggressively so. It might be warning us of danger or functioning as a border sentry for a portion of the woods. It was remarked to us that it may be more playful than militant. Indeed, it may be the forest's defensive end or starting shortstop. Either way—spiritual warrior or fun-loving athlete—it is a distinctive physical presence.

UNTAMED P.86: Freest of free spirits, the wolf howls as daylight wanes.

ASPIRING P.88: We observe that spiritual ascension requires dedication, commitment and unyielding concentration if we wish to attain greater understanding.

DUTIFUL P.90: This sentry is always on alert, eyes wide open and weapon over the shoulder, patrolling the forest for signs of danger.

DRAMATIC P.92: A non-stop performance of an extraordinary closing number. This tree spirit has our complete attention.

WHIMSICAL P.94: Looking a bit like Thing from the Addams Family, this being peeks out from behind the flowing lines with a happy-go-lucky attitude. It's a little silly and a little ugly, in the most strikingly beautiful way. Is it this?... or is it that? It's pretty much whatever we want him/her to be and that's just how he/she likes it. All that matters is that everyone is having a nice time.

OBSESSED P.96: Try as he might (and try he has for some period of time), season after season, year after year... he just can't leave it alone.

HAND OF GOD P.98: OK, so this is a bit of an extravagant trick, the kind that trees like to play. The real beauty of this massive tree wasn't apparent until we saw the second picture in the series. Our friend Dennis Edgeton was bicycling across Louisiana when he came upon this reminder of our place in the universe and the immense importance of perspective.

PASSIONATE P.100: Wrapped around each other in a *passionate* embrace, it is impossible to tell whether they are two or one. Either way, they are one. Indeed, they are so rapt that they express the timelessness of love, the beauty of their surroundings, the time of the season and all that is.

MISCHIEVOUS P.102: A joke a minute; a lovable smart aleck who takes nothing too seriously. Never dull, always fun, even when the joke's on us. Pass the cigars. Groucho Marx reincarnated.

SPELLBOUND P.104: Witchlike in appearance, she floats through the forest in search of…whatever it is she's looking for. We swear we've seen her in different places on the hills and in the marshy flats.

STUBBORN P.106: No matter what happens, regardless of external circumstances, nothing will deter these two from their objective. That's just how it's going to be and you're not going to change their mind(s).

AGONIZED P.108: Edvard Munch's "The Scream" revisited in nature.

WILY P.110: Crouching in the grass, ears perked up, the *wily* coyote sleeps with one eye open while contemplating his nighttime chicanery.

CONNECTED P.112: In close proximity from germination through adolescence, these trees experienced a spiritual attraction so great that it manifested physically. Or perhaps it was the other way around. They seemed preoccupied so we didn't ask.

ORNERY P.114: With scraggly beard and generally disheveled appearance, he's heard yodeling his lungs out at all hours of the windiest days and nights around the lake. He's high-spirited and good-spirited most of the time. This is his woods and he'll do what's necessary to keep it that way.

ATTENTIVE P.116: Never mind the seemingly unreasonable violence of the Big Storm of 2009. Life goes on without regret or resentment. We stand at attention to welcome the new day with all the optimism and enthusiasm in the world; we know the best is yet to come.

BRAVE P.118: Bearing the scar of a great battle or tumultuous event, you can count on this strong, steady survivor standing watch at the edge of the woods. He knows who comes in and who goes out.

CLUMSY P.120: Okay, this one's up for grabs. Everybody sees something different. But here goes: This powerful, well-armored warrior is patrolling the forest, possibly in pursuit of the occasional ne'er do well (maybe Mischievous, who's just given him the old hot foot) when... *Oops!* ...he trips and falls flat on his face. He's embarrassed and wishes we hadn't seen this, but what are you gonna' do?

DANGEROUS P.122: Peril can be where you least expect it, like the snake that sits atop the woodpile. She looks threatening but she is not malicious. Upon closer scrutiny, there is something lovely about her. Her purpose is to protect those who trust her to do so. The forest has a way of looking after itself.

RADIANT P.124: Today's glorious sunshine and beautiful blue sky was made for this beauty. Surrounding trees seemed to know and appreciate that fact by giving way to accommodate the dazzling show.

NOCTURNAL P.126: There is something bat-like and vampirish about this creature. It might be fun to go back late at night and see if it is still there. But only if you go with us.

RELAXED P.128: Sunbathers yawning. No worries here.

RELENTLESS P.130: Perhaps a long lost cousin of the great car-eating tree we once observed several states away, these imposing limbs set out decades ago to crawl across the landscape all the way to… wherever it wants to go.

SURPRISED P.132: What would life be if we really had seen everything, if we considered ourselves so experienced as to become incapable of amazement?

AWAKENED P.134: It is the prerogative of the older ones to wake up a little slowly. With the earthen blanket pulled up around its neck in the late autumn air, it gives forth a magnificent yawn and well deserved stretch. After we named this photo for the book, a friend of ours said he would have named it Watcher, to which we replied, "Huh?" He laughed and responded, "Look closely. When you see it, it will send chills up your spine."

Now, we can't look at this photo without seeing the human face peering out at us. In fact, we can't take our eyes off of him. It goes to show that no matter how familiar we are with our surroundings, 'we see what we see.'

PURPOSEFUL P.136: We named this one 'vacuous' for the longest time, but how on earth could a spiritually hollow being grow to such impressive height and distinctive beauty? Will, reason, love and other purposes we're not privileged to know are driving this tree toward the heavens.

WHOO-HOO! P.138: "I love this forest!" Enthusiasm is all you need to have a really good time.

SATISFIED P.140: From early morning to noontime light, this Muppet-like spirit's countenance changes from a sneer to a smirk; but always, by the afternoon there appears a soft smile and the assurance that the day ultimately brings contentment and satisfaction.

MIGHTY P.142: This Herculean evergreen looks as if it could support the very universe itself.

BEST FRIENDS P.144: These two are so close in spirit that they never tire of each other's company. Arm in arm they go laughing down the street every day, making this a very happy neighborhood.

GENEROUS P.146: When one is as beautiful and expansive as this, the natural thing for a mature spirit to do is share the bounty with all who may benefit from it.

DISCUSSION GUIDE

Have you felt it? That incredible connection with trees? It's difficult to describe but you know when it's happening. The following questions are for parents, teachers, book club participants or individuals who would like to expand on the pictures, captions and quotes in this book. This guide is merely a starting point. It is my hope that these questions will spark many more of your own.

- Which tree picture from the book is your favorite and why?

- Which quote from the book is your favorite and why?

- Tell a story about a time in your life when one of the photos in the book expresses how you felt.

- Choose three authors quoted in the book and report on their background and lives. Any surprises? Why did you pick those three?

- The quotes from the book are more than 100 years old. In what ways do these quotes still apply today?

- Choose three of your favorite quotes and find more recent quotes to go with these pictures/captions.

- Choose three of the one-word captions and look up the definitions of these words. Any surprises?

- Has this book changed the way you see trees and if so, how?

- Pick a tree picture from the book for which you personally did not see what the author saw, based on the author's description in the appendix (or her choice of caption and quote). Tell us what you saw in the picture and what caption you would have given it.

- When was the first time you felt a connection to the trees? Were you a young child or was it later in life? Describe the tree and the connection you felt.

- If you were a tree, what would you look like?

- What if trees had human eyes? What might they have witnessed in their lifetimes? What stories could they tell? What changes might have happened while they stood where they are?

- Draw a picture of your favorite tree (real or imagined).

- Tell us about your favorite tree. Is it still standing? Was it a tree from your childhood? Where is it and why do you feel connected to it?

- What is the purpose of trees in this world? Why are they here?

- In what other forms of nature do you see characters or faces?

- In what ways can trees be "teachers of transitions" in our lives?

SHARE YOUR THOUGHTS

The author has described trees as dynamic sculptures of nature and one of our most raw and natural art forms. Observe a tree over a six month time frame. What has changed about this tree during that time? Describe these changes.

    When you look at trees—you will see what you see. I invite you to share what you see by submitting your pictures to the photo gallery on the website: *www.personalitreesbook.com*

Thanks so much for taking this walk with me. I look forward to seeing what you see!
— Joan

    See *www.personalitreesbook.com* website and send your tree pictures to the Gallery on the Personalitreesbook.com website.

    Join as friends on the PersonaliTrees **Facebook** and **Twitter** pages.

    E-mail your comments to *boss@beingofsoundspirit.com*

ACKNOWLEDGEMENTS

ANY PROJECT WORTH DOING typically cannot be done in a vacuum. It often takes points of view and frames of reference well beyond one person's own line of vision. I am most grateful to the following people for their help and support:

My sister, Mary Hanish (Moon) for harmonizing with me not only in music but in writing as well, along with sisters Lois Lenz and Marcia Klostermann for your unwavering support and editorial help. Bruce and Colleen Rieks for naming this book and your faithful friendship!

For participating in numerous focus groups and tolerating the many requests for suggestions, thank you to my kids, Michelle Gravel and Paul Sonderegger, Ben and Rachel Digmann, Matt Gravel and my sisters Theresa Prier, Jane Murillo, and niece, Leah Kestel. Thanks also, to Kristi Musser, Dennis Edgeton, Martha Edgeton, Karin Leonard, Bob and Jovita Long, Bart Rieks, Vicki Newell, Margie Skahill, Jean Vaux, Diane Roberts and Marsha Fisher.

Heartfelt thanks also to: Bud and Barb Ketels, Allan Hunter, Cat Bennett and Kat Tansey, Michaela Rich, Curt Hanson, Alex and Taylor Hanson, Glenda Wilson & Jim Boyland, Ann Raisch, Wayne Adams, Rosanne and Don Primus, Greg Van Fosson, Chuck and Patty Holley, the Breakfast Group, my Beckman high school girlfriends and everyone who loves trees.

And finally, my deepest gratitude and sincere thanks to the staff at Findhorn Press for trusting the universe and publishing PersonaliTrees and HumaniTrees. Thierry, Sabine, Carol, Mieke, Gail and Cynthia— you are the best! And to Damian Keenan for working your magic!

FINDHORN PRESS

Life Changing Books

For a complete catalogue,
please contact:

Findhorn Press
117-121 High Street,
Forres IV36 1AB,
Scotland, UK

t +44 (0)1309 690582
f +44 (0)131 777 2711
e info@findhornpress.com

or consult our catalogue online
(with secure order facility) on
www.findhornpress.com

For information on the Findhorn Foundation:
www.findhorn.org